# WHEN THE EARTH MOVES

**SANDRA DOWNS**

TWENTY-FIRST CENTURY BOOKS
BROOKFIELD, CONNECTICUT

Library of Congress Cataloging-in-Publication Data
Downs, Sandra.
When the Earth moves / Sandra Friend Downs.
p.  cm. — (Exploring planet earth)
Includes bibliographical references and index.
Summary: Describes and explains the geological phenomena
of earthquakes, landslides, sinkholes, quicksand, and avalanches.
ISBN 0-7613-1412-1 (lib. bdg.)
1. Earth movements—Juvenile literature. [1. Earth movements.]
I. Title.  II. Series.
QE598.3.D68  2000    551—dc21  99-23728  CIP  AC

Published by Twenty-First Century Books
A Division of The Millbrook Press, Inc.
2 Old New Milford Road, Brookfield, Connecticut 06804
www.millbrookpress.com

Book Design: Victoria Monks
Photo Research: Sabina Dowell

Cover photograph courtesy of  Woodfin Camp & Associates (© Mike Yamashita)
Photographs courtesy of Liaison Agency: pp. 8 (© Piero Pomponi), 13 (© Ed Lallo), 26, 46 (© Brant
Ward/*San Francisco Chronicle*); Visuals Unlimited: pp. 10 (© William J. Weber), 11 (© George Herben);
AP/Wide World Photos: pp. 15, 18, 29; U. S. Geological Survey: pp. 16, 35, 36; Animals Animals/Earth
Scenes: pp. 19 (© Michael Habicht), 44 (© Fred Whitehead); NGS/Image Collection: p. 21 (© Steve
Raymer); Woodfin Camp & Associates: pp. 23 (© David Cupp), 24 (© David Cupp), 41 (© Chuck
Nacke), 50 (© Leif Skoogfors); Science Source/Photo Researchers: p. 30 (© Calvin Larsen); © Archive
Photos: p. 38 (Reuters/Eriko Sugita); Natural Bridge of Virginia: p. 42; *Youngstown Vindicator*: p. 49

# CONTENTS

# WHEN THE
# EARTH
# MOVES

**"I dreamt that the house fell down.** Where's Mommy and Daddy?"

Stunned and covered from head to foot in dust, six-year-old Akin Sirnen was one of the fortunate ones. Rescue workers dug him out of a collapsed building in Golcuk, Turkey, a day after one of the world's worst earthquake disasters. Others were not so lucky.

While people in Turkey slept on August 17, 1999, the ground shook. Apartment buildings collapsed. Water and sewer pipes broke, spilling their contents onto the streets. Telephone cables snapped. Bridges twisted and fell. Minarets toppled. In just seconds, tens of thousands of people disappeared under rubble. More than 15,000 people died.

Earthquakes threaten Turkey frequently. It sits on the North Anatolian Fault, which, like California's San Andreas Fault, slips westward an average of 0.138 inches (35 millimeters) each year. In 1939 an earthquake struck the city of Erzincan, killing 33,000 people. Since then, tremendous earthquakes have moved west along this fault line toward Istanbul, Turkey's most densely populated city. Izmit lies only 55 miles (88 kilometers) southeast of Istanbul.

At 7.4 on the Richter scale, the Izmit earthquake was one of the strongest in modern history. Turkish engineers worked with California scientists on earthquake-proof building design, but there was little enforcement of building codes in Turkey. The crowded cities of Golcuk and Izmit were reduced to ruins.

*Rescue workers look for survivors of the August 17, 1999, Turkish earthquake that registered 7.4 on the Richter scale and killed over 15,000 people. One month later, on September 21, 1999, Taiwan experienced a 7.6 earthquake with over 2,100 casualties. There were actually fewer earthquakes in 1999 than in an average year, but they occurred in heavily populated places.*

Without an earthquake preparedness plan, the Turkish government struggled with the rescue effort required. Surviving family members and friends used shovels, picks, and hands to dig the injured out of the rubble. Rescue workers came from around the globe, bringing medical supplies and dogs to sniff out people trapped under collapsed buildings.

The risk of future earthquakes remains high. But the fortunate survivors, like Akin, will be able to rebuild their lives—and plan ahead for Turkey's next big earthquake.

When the earth moves and people are affected, it makes for big news. Newspapers and television show us the results: twisted bridges in the aftermath of an earthquake, houses sliding down slippery slopes of mud, and lava pouring through city streets.

Yet our earth is in constant motion. The ground beneath our feet never rests, never stays the same. The very surface of the earth is broken up into a jigsaw puzzle of continental plates. Riding on currents of hot magma deep within the earth, they bump and push and scrape as they collide. In many places, these plates slide and grind softly against each other, releasing pressure gradually, cracking the ground in a fault. In other places, they lock up, generating intense stress that can only be released through an earthquake.

Powerful forces creating sudden motion are interconnected. Earthquakes can make volcanoes belch ash, gas clouds, and lava; cause the ground to subside, separate, and create massive landslides and avalanches. Volcanic eruptions can cause earthquakes and landslides. And a landslide can start an earthquake!

When we walk around outdoors, we see evidence of the earth's constant movement. Rocks fall to the bottom of cliffs. Cracks in the road open up into potholes. Rain carries away soil, sculpting little gullies into a hillside. Rivers rise, eating at the soil along their banks. Mountains shrink as streams cut deeper into rock. The same processes that created our dramatic landscapes—from the Grand Canyon to the Appalachian Mountains—are still at work today, gradually forming new landscapes for the future.

Not all earth movement happens suddenly. But the sudden, dangerous movements—the ones that make the news—are set up by long, slow processes that eventually trigger an explosive ending.

## CREEPING GROUND

As a loose particle of soil warms up in the afternoon sun, it expands and lifts upward. Then, as the sun goes down, the particle cools and contracts, settling into a new spot. Plant roots trap particles of soil, holding them firmly against the hillside. But a little rain, or wind, or the hurried footsteps of a mouse can pop that piece of soil out of its comfy spot and send it on a journey toward the bottom of the hill. Gravity makes sure that every particle of soil will eventually end up at the lowest point it can reach. This slow process of earth movement is called soil creep.

You can see the effects of soil creep if you look carefully at any hillside. Trees tend to bend downward as the soil holding their roots heads downhill. Miniature landslides, inches high, form where the ground

*Soil creep in action. Over the years this hut has moved close to the edge of the hill. A foundation can help to anchor a house in place.*

cover—the layer of plants and grasses whose dense roots hold down soil—is scarce. Tilted telephone poles and fence posts show the effects of the constant, gradual process of soil creep.

Rock creep occurs when fragments of rock move slowly downhill. Water and ice help to make the rocks more slippery, so they flow over each other. Plant roots break up bigger rocks into smaller pieces, and gravity pulls them down. Like soil particles, rocks can move ever so slowly by expansion and contraction. Often, soil creep and rock creep take place on the same hillside.

As weathering and erosion pry rocks from cliff faces, the rocks fall down and accumulate in piles at the bottom of the cliff. When a lot of rocks fall in one place, they create what is called a talus pile. The pile builds up in a triangular shape against the cliff. Eventually, the pile grows too large, and it starts to slowly flow outward.

Most talus piles we see along roadcuts contain small fragments of rock, smaller than your hand. But in some parts of the world, winter

*This rock glacier is slowly on its way down the mountain, although it could turn into something dangerous in the right conditions—a landslide!*

freezes cause ice to wedge huge blocks of rock off the sides of mountains. These large blocks create massive talus piles. The piles begin to flow like a glacier, spreading out and away from the original point where the pile began. Rock glaciers are a common occurrence in high upper mountain valleys. Unlike a dangerous and sudden landslide, a rock glacier follows a slow and predictable descent down a mountain. However, if the rock glacier is disturbed by an earthquake or soaked with a large quantity of water, it can turn into a landslide.

## LAID TO WASTE

Mass movement is the general term used to describe the downward flow of rocks and soil due to gravity. Many factors affect how quickly any given amount of material will slide down a hill. The steepness of the slope is an important consideration, along with the amount of ground cover that is helping to anchor the material down. Rainfall has an immediate effect on downhill motion: It accelerates the process by making the soil heavier and slippery. Rock formations and fallen logs can act like dams, holding back soil from flowing downhill. A footpath created to climb a mountain will accelerate erosion.

When soaked by a heavy rain, masses of loose soil often break free and form an earthflow. This occurs most readily where there is thick, saturated soil on top of a layer of impermeable bedrock or clay. An earthflow moves very slowly and short distances, as the soaked soil slides along on top of the dry layer below it. The soil will look broken up, full of cracks and crevices, and the end of the flow forms a raised spot called a toe.

A mudflow occurs when soil is so saturated with water that it flows like a sticky stream. Mudflows occur in places where there is no ground cover, as along an eroded highway embankment, or in a farmer's newly plowed field. Mudflows and earthflows are the junior cousins of mudslides and landslides.

Slumping occurs when a mass of soil or rock breaks away from its original spot and slides to another, lower spot on the hillside. You can make a slump: If you scoop some ice cream in a tablespoon, and tip the spoon forward, the ice cream will slide partly off the spoon. A slump, when it falls forward, leaves a little cliff behind (called a scarp) at the point where the soil breaks away. Like an earthflow, a slump has a toe indicating where it ends.

## GROWING STONES

When winter comes to northern regions, it unleashes a powerful underground force called frost heaving. When the temperature of the soil dips below 32°F (0°C), water trapped under the ground freezes. If the surface warms up a little—perhaps because of being in the warm sun—some of the ice closer to the surface turns back into water and is drawn to the surface like a paper towel soaking up a spill. This movement of water freezing and thawing, pushing up and down, can exert a tremendous lifting force. The force of frost heaving can even snap tree roots and shift building foundations! And frost heaving is responsible for the potholes and cracks in pavement in cold climates.

Frost heaving pushes rocks toward the surface, as well. After the spring thaw, new stones appear near the surface of the cracked ground. Some of the stones may have traveled several feet. So every year, farmers and backyard gardeners must dig a new load of stones out of the ground in order to get ready for spring planting.

From the massive crunching of continental plates to the tiny bounces of a particle of soil rolling downhill, the earth beneath our feet is constantly in motion. Most earth movements are slow and harmless, escaping our attention. It's when these movements accelerate and break free that we begin to take notice.

*Frost heaves start many road cracks and potholes. Once the surface is disturbed, automobile traffic speeds up wear on the road.*

# 2 SLIPS AND SLIDES

A loud rumble came from the hills above the tiny coal mining village of Aberfan, Wales. It was October 21, 1966, and students at Pantglas Junior High hummed songs from their Friday assembly as they walked back to their classrooms. Up on the mountain above, a pile of waste rock at the coal mine started to tumble. Miners watched in horror, unable to use their broken telephone to sound a warning. The foggy noontime air obscured the raging river of rock that streamed down the mountain.

According to one eight-year-old student, Gaynor Minett: "It was a tremendous rumbling sound. Everyone just froze in their seats. I just managed to get up, and I reached the end of my desk when the sound got louder and nearer, until I could see the black out of the window."

Then Gaynor and the rest of his classmates were buried in the terrible onrush of rock that crushed the school and twenty houses in its path. Within minutes, hundreds of people rushed to the scene. They dug into the rough rock but could save only half of the children. Aberfan lost 144 people, 116 of them students at Pantglas Junior High, to the terror of a sudden landslide.

## CREEP THAT WON'T SLOW DOWN

Landslides and rockslides occur suddenly, often with devastating consequences. Farmlands and forests disappear. Telephone and electric

When people daydream about living in Malibu, they forget how often the Pacific Coast Highway is blocked by landslides.

wires snap, and pipes buried underground can break. Tunnels can collapse under the unexpected added weight of a mass of rock. Entire towns have disappeared under tons of soil. Roads can be blocked. California's Pacific Coast Highway might hold the record for the most closures due to landslides. It has been blocked more than 300 times in ten years!

*It was more than just a matter of clearing the road after this landslide—the highway was rebuilt around the slide.*

Water suffers when landslides hit. Reservoirs suddenly filled with rock can rush over a dam, creating a threatening flood. In 1963 a mass of limestone blocks suddenly slid from the slope of Mount Toc in the Italian Alps into the Vaiont Reservoir. The 260 million cubic meters (9,182 million cubic feet) of stone caused a wave 100 meters (328 feet) high to jump over the dam. Almost 2,000 people died as the wave crashed over the dam, destroying towns in the valley below. Landslides can dam up an existing river, making a temporary lake. The unstable material eventually will break apart, suddenly spilling a flood of water into the valleys below. The sudden impact of soil into water can also cause giant waves, affecting shorelines miles away. Landslides along the Norwegian fjords create massive swells in the sea, driving waves more than 100 feet (30 meters) high against the shore.

Landslides occur underwater on a regular basis. These submarine landslides fall off the continental shelf and flow down the sides of seafloor volcanoes. Massive piles of rocks surround the island of Hawaii, deep underwater. At least fifteen different landslides pushed these rocks as much as 150 miles (240 kilometers) from where they first fell! Geologists think that the volcanoes that created the island eventually fell apart in massive landslides.

Landslides of rock, called rockslides, move rapidly. Often whole cliffs collapse in a free fall of rock. The most destructive rockslide in history occurred on January 10, 1962, when 6 million cubic yards (4.6 million cubic meters) of rocks and ice suddenly slid down from the summit of Nevada de Huascarán in Peru. In only 15 minutes, the massive flow traveled 11 miles (18 kilometers), crushing seven villages. No one knows the exact reason for this rockslide, but it wasn't triggered by an earthquake.

You've probably seen road signs warning about falling rocks. Because rockslides often occur along roadcuts, highway departments use special measures to prevent damage to cars. In California, highway workers climb steep cliffs and knock down boulders. They intentionally blast whole hillsides apart to loosen dangerous rock while a road is closed. In many rockslide-prone places, strong steel nets protect highways from falling rocks.

Landslides of clay are especially treacherous because they move quickly. One of the largest and most destructive clay slides occurred near the village of Vaerdalen in Norway, in 1893. A stream had eroded

*This rockslide near Pittsburgh, Pennsylvania, crushed three vehicles and killed two people.*

into a layer of very soft clay. As the water flowed into the clay, the entire mass of 55 million cubic meters (1,942 million cubic feet) slid down into a river valley. This rapid flow of wet clay dammed a large river, destroyed 22 farms, and killed 111 people in just 30 minutes.

*Steel netting is hung along Route 101 in Washington State to keep falling rock fragments off the highway.*

## WHY DOES THE LAND SLIDE?

Erosion is the starting point for every landslide. In the natural processes of mass movement, rocks and soil roll downhill. In the long term, gravity will pull all of the soil and rocks down a mountainside. But when they occur suddenly, they're called landslides. So what triggers the sudden crash or flow of debris into a valley?

Earthquakes and tremors, vibrating soil and rock, can start a landslide or mudslide. Soil liquefaction can happen, causing loose soil to flow downhill like water. Tremors can also liquefy clay, making it behave like grease. The layer of earth on top of the affected clay will simply slide over it. During very severe earthquakes, entire mountain ranges have sudden landslides. A major earthquake in Tibet in 1950 caused almost every south-facing slope of the Himalayan Mountains— more than 12,000 square miles (31,080 square kilometers) of land—to be completely stripped of forests by landslides.

Volcanoes can create landslides as they spew out fresh lava and ash. One of the most terrible volcanic landslides of this century happened in Colombia in 1985, killing 20,000 people in just a few minutes. When the volcano, Nevado del Ruiz, exploded, its heat instantly melted a snowcap on top of the mountain. The rush of water mixed with ash and flowed down the mountain at more than 30 miles (48 kilometers) per hour, engulfing villages 15 feet (4.5 meters) deep in sticky muck. Said one observer: "From the air, it looked as if a giant load of wet concrete had been spilled down a lush, fertile valley."

Such muddy volcanic outbursts are known as lahars. They contain a combination of ashes, soil, rocks, and fluids that flow down the side of a volcano. Lahars can flow up to 60 miles (97 kilometers) per hour, spreading out over a wide area. The highest active volcano on earth is Cotopaxi, in Ecuador. Since it's almost 20,000 feet (6,100 meters) tall, its lahars have flowed as far as 200 miles (320 kilometers)!

In populated areas prone to volcanic activity, special efforts are made to protect towns from lahars and lava. The slopes of Mount Usu, Japan, have dozens of concrete "check dams" crossing the mountain's natural drainage paths. These dams help to protect the city of Hokkaido by slowing down and channeling the lahars. Although these dams may fail, they give the people in the city extra time to evacuate. Similarly, during an eruption in 1991, the Italian Army used explosives to divert lava from Mount Etna away from villages. The U.S. Marines

The lahar from an eruption of Nevado del Ruiz, a volcano in Colombia, devastated the town of Armero. Covering 16 square miles (42 square kilometers), the moving wall of mud and ash struck at 11 P.M., when most people were asleep.

21

dropped concrete dams from helicopters to stop the lahars. Their joint efforts saved the village of Zafferana.

## GIVING US THE SLIP

In cold regions—including the tops of high mountains—some of the soil stays permanently frozen. This layer, called permafrost, can't soak up any of the rain or melted snow that seeps into the soil above it. The thawed soil above the permafrost always gets very soggy, or water-logged. This layer tends to slip and flow in a process called solifluction. Any soil layer prone to solifluction will slip slowly downhill, accelerating as the slope of the hill increases or the amount of water in the soil increases. Solifluction can occur anywhere that water can't seep deeper into the ground—because of permafrost, or solid bedrock, or layers of soil that are already too saturated.

Mudflows, which move much more quickly than landslides, start with solifluction. Entire hillsides can collapse in a wall of mud if the soil is waterlogged. Heavy rains can turn soil into a liquid mass if there is nowhere else for the water to go. Mudflows flow like liquid, pouring through houses and carrying away cars.

In May 1998, about 6 inches (15 centimeters) of rain fell on Italy's Mount Sarno in two days. Torrents of mud quickly engulfed the city of Sarno, at the bottom of the mountain. Mud burst through the hospital, pouring through windows and doors and flowing down staircases. Patients escaped by climbing out windows on their bedsheets! The rushing mud dragged one five-story building at least 500 yards (457 meters) down the street. In just three days, 1,600 people lost their homes, and 55 people died.

Mudflows are due to insufficient ground cover. In California, bare hillsides and rain are a recipe for disaster. Wildfires raging through the mountains ensure that there is very little ground cover to fight the effects of solifluction. We see the same scenes every year on the evening news: houses sliding down hills and mud pouring down roads. Mudslides occur so frequently in the San Gabriel Mountains that special pits the size of football fields and large dams have been built on hillsides to protect the neighborhoods below. So much soil and rock slides into these pits that they are mined as a source of sand and gravel! The company that does this has never been able to empty the pits before they start filling back up again.

## WHAT YOU CAN DO ABOUT MUDFLOWS

Try to find out if your neighborhood is prone to mudflows. Do you live at the bottom of a steep hill? Does it have ground cover? Has there ever been a mudflow in your neighborhood? If so, the most important thing you can do is to avoid sleeping in lower-floor rooms that face the hills. These are the rooms that will fill up with mud if a sudden mudflow occurs.

*Avalanche! As more people build back-country houses and visit wilderness areas in winter, we're discovering how common avalanches are.*

23

*Airborne powder avalanches can be triggered by noise, such as the slam of a car door.*

To know whether your family should evacuate, pay attention to how much rain is falling. If more than 3 inches (8 centimeters) of rain falls in a day, or more than 1/4 inch (6 millimeters) of rain falls in an hour, the soil may be waterlogged enough to trigger a mudflow.

If you notice cracks in the hillside, trees tilting due to rapid soil creep, or actual earthflows forming, call 911 or your local emergency number. Be ready to evacuate quickly!

## AVALANCHE: SNOW ON THE MOVE

The Alps, a tall mountain range lying between Germany, Austria, France, and Italy, has had a long history of avalanches. Switzerland lies right in the middle of the Alps and has lost hundreds of villages to crushing walls of snow.

The earliest description of an avalanche came from the Greek writer Strabo, who between 64 and 36 B.C. wrote a geography book about his travels. Of avalanches in the Alps, he wrote: "Layers of ice that slide down from above—enormous layers capable of intercepting a whole caravan."

When Hannibal's army crossed the Alps in 218 B.C., he lost thousands of men, horses, and elephants to avalanches. According to one observer, "Detached snow drags the men into the abyss." When Napoleon's army marched through the Alps, his chief marshal wrote to say, "Avalanches had swallowed entire squadrons." During World War I and World War II, troops intentionally caused avalanches by firing shells into snowy slopes. In 1916 more than 3,000 Austrian soldiers were killed in under 48 hours by avalanches triggered as weapons.

Avalanches occur randomly. Sometimes they wipe out an entire village. Sometimes they sweep away one house. On rare occasions, avalanches have been helpful. By flattening forests and carrying them downhill, an avalanche brought a wealth of timber to a poor village.

Since the Swiss have had so many centuries in which to study avalanches, they've been able to reduce the danger to their homes. Special lean-to roofs called galleries cover roads and railroad tracks along avalanche-prone mountainsides. Defensive latticework fences slow down the onrush of snow, buying time for people to evacuate buildings below. Reinforced concrete and steel shutters shield buildings thought to lie in the potential path of an avalanche. Certain valleys always seem to have avalanches. These avalanche paths, called couloirs, are well mapped. No one lives in a couloir. In many mountain towns in the United States, it is illegal to build anywhere in an avalanche zone.

Today, avalanches are primarily a threat to mountain climbers and skiers. At least 80 percent of all avalanche victims are tourists enjoying winter sports. In 50 years, more than 1,000 people died from avalanches in the Swiss Alps. In the case of skiers, most deaths occur because the skiers ignored posted warnings to avoid certain slopes. Mountain climbers face more danger from avalanches than from falling. In the western United States, more than 100,000 avalanches occur annually,

*An avalanche in Zurs, Austria, in February 1999. The Alps had a surprising number of avalanches in the first two months of 1999. An avalanche in Galtür, Austria, killed twenty-three people. The year began with unusually large amounts of snow and high winds that created great drifts.*

killing about 25 people a year. Most of these avalanches are in the backcountry, triggered by skiers, climbers, and hikers. But avalanches can occur in populated areas, too. Road crews in Alaska must constantly monitor the Seward Highway for potential problems. To prevent avalanches from sweeping down and crushing motorists, the road crews use artillery fire to trigger intentional avalanches, which they then clear off the road.

Gravity, snowfall, and temperature all create the potential for avalanches. A steep slope makes it more likely that an avalanche will occur. Multiple layers of snow, settling on top of each other, also set the stage for collapse. When temperatures change, snow begins to change. It may melt and reform into ice crystals, or compress into a hard slab. Very frequently, a layer of crunchy frost on top of the snow gets buried and compressed by the next snowfall. The frost layer is weak, filled with slippery ice crystals, and tends to melt easily. As the upper layer of snow gets undermined, it is prone to collapse. If an upper layer is heavier than a lower layer, it will slip off and fall.

There are two types of avalanches. In an airborne powder avalanche, clouds of snow lift off the mountainside and flow down in a gigantic burst of wind. Racing at more than 200 miles (320 kilometers) per hour, this snow-filled blast of wind can flatten forests and buildings. An airborne powder avalanche can be triggered by a footstep, a blast of wind, or a loud noise.

A ground avalanche is a collapse of wet snow in a massive downhill slide. Ground avalanches usually carry along rocks and soil, creating big snowballs. They move slowly down well-known couloirs. Snow melting due to spring thaw launches most ground avalanches.

Avalanche researchers carefully study snow. They still can't tell why some slopes that never had an avalanche suddenly do . . . or why five skiers can cross a slope, and the slope collapses under the last person. But research, particularly in the Swiss Alps, has led to many safety measures to aid skiers.

Ski patrols always scout the snowy slopes for avalanche potential, posting warnings when a ski trail should not be used. When the slopes are clear, they use explosives to trigger small "safe" avalanches to offset the danger of larger ones.

Beacons help rescuers find skiers who are buried in a sudden avalanche. These beacons haven't always been successful, since people can be suffocated under the snow. Now, a new device called an Avalanche Balloon System (ABS), attached to a skier like a parachute, helps a skier float near the top of the flow during an avalanche. Its bright-red color attracts rescuers.

## WHAT YOU CAN DO

If you ski, you are at risk of being caught in an avalanche. Be sure to follow all recommended preparations at the ski resort, including wearing a beacon or an ABS. Never ignore posted warnings that a ski slope is unsafe!

Landslides, mudflows, and avalanches all cause the ground to move suddenly downhill. When they shuffle the earth's surface without our knowing about it, they are natural forces acting as vast sculptors of land. When they affect people, they are natural disasters. We can often defend ourselves against them, putting up obstacles like dams and fences to deflect their flow. But when the earth starts to move under our feet, we are caught by surprise.

Just before sunrise on January 17, 1995, the ground started to shake under the busy city of Kobe, Japan. Bridges fell in twisted wrecks. Trains, thrown from their tracks, looked like sprawling snakes. Elevated highways fell down, dropping trucks and cars into buildings below. Homes, apartments, and office buildings collapsed—190,000 buildings in all—trapping thousands of people under piles of brick and metal.

Japan has a long history of earthquakes, because it sits on the edge of a continental plate. Schoolchildren have earthquake drills. Buildings are built to special standards to withstand shocks. Because of the country's preparedness, no one expected the terrible mess that the Great Hanshin Earthquake created. Kobe, Japan's largest port, sat very near the epicenter of this 6.9 magnitude quake. The tremors lasted less than a minute, but they left 300,000 people homeless and 5,500 dead. A million people had no water or electricity. Luckily, the quake hit before people were on their way to work, or many more people would have died.

Earthquakes are a shocking reminder of how little control we have over the vast geologic forces that shape our planet. Reporter James Hopper, writing about the survivors of the great San Francisco earthquake of 1906, saw that people carried "a hurt expression—not one of physical pain, but rather one of injured sensibilities, as if some trusted

*The Hanshin Expressway lies on its side after an earthquake shook Nishinomiya. It's hard to imagine the power of a quake that can tip over a highway as though it were a toy.*

friend had suddenly wronged them." There is nothing we can do to prevent earthquakes. But by learning about them, we can learn how best to protect ourselves.

*The vast amount of water contained by Hoover Dam has a measurable effect on the earth under and surrounding the area. Seismic activity varies with the level of the lake.*

## TREMBLING EARTH

If you've ever stood near a busy road, you may have noticed that the ground shakes when a big truck goes by. The motion of such a large, heavy mass creates a tremor, a small shake of the ground that radiates out from the truck's tires. If you stomp on the sidewalk, your footsteps will create a small tremor that might scare a few ants.

Tremors occur constantly in the earth's crust. They are seismic waves, small but measurable movements that can be tracked to predict the possibility of a large earthquake. While tremors can signal deep earth movements, they aren't always caused by these movements.

When miners set off explosions inside the earth to expand a tunnel in a mine, the explosion will cause a tremor. Tremors can also occur in response to the collapse of a cavern roof or mine tunnel. When large masses of rock fall underground, they create seismic waves.

A strong impact on the earth's surface can generate tremors. In 1908 a large meteorite exploded over the woods near

Tunguska, Siberia. Although it was more than 6 miles (10 kilometers) in the air, it flattened a huge forest and created seismic waves recorded all across Europe.

Water pressure has been known to trigger tremors. Soon after the Hoover Dam was completed and Lake Mead was filled with water, seismologists (people who study tremors and earthquakes) started recording seismic waves that seemed to be related to the water-level changes in the lake. Water adds pressure to the existing strain in a rock, weakening it. Engineers have noticed this problem behind some of the world's largest dams, such as the Aswan High Dam in Egypt. Where once there was never a seismic reading, now there are constant, small tremors.

Volcanic activity has been the source of many tremors. A sudden upward burst of magma under pressure sends out seismic waves. People who live in the shadow of Mount Vesuvius and Mount Etna in Italy look to tremors as a warning sign of a potential volcanic eruption.

The intensity of a sudden, severe landslide can create seismic waves, as well. On April 25, 1974, along the Mantaro River in Peru, a landslide containing 1.6 cubic kilometers of rock slid for 4 miles (7 kilometers), causing tremors up to 4.5 in magnitude on the Richter scale. In 1911 a landslide in the Pamir Mountains of Russia showed up on seismographs in Moscow, more than 1,864 miles (3,000 kilometers) away!

Even the weather can cause tremors! Strong winds, rushing across the face of the earth, generate enough friction to constantly nudge the earth's crust a tiny bit. This causes the earth to constantly vibrate like a ringing bell.

## EARTHQUAKES: THE DEADLIEST SHAKES

Because of the memorable destruction that accompanies most earthquakes, they've been newsworthy items all through human history.

"A frightful disaster, surpassing anything related either in legend or authentic history," wrote historian Ammianus Marcellinus of the massive earthquake that rocked the Mediterranean in A.D. 35. Centered offshore from the major port of Kourion, Cyprus, the quake destroyed the city and sent tsunamis—earthquake-generated walls of water—in all directions. These killed "many thousands of men by drowning," from Alexandria, Egypt, to the southern Peleponnesus of Greece.

People tried to invent reasons for the occurrence of earthquakes. In Hindu legend the world sat on the shoulders of elephants, and one of the elephants must have kneeled. Siberians blamed the sled dog of their god (who carried the earth on a sled) for stopping to scratch fleas.

The Mainas, in Peru, came up with a lifesaving earthquake tale. They thought that when their god visited the earth to count his people, his footsteps caused the tremors. Each person would rush outdoors to say, "I'm here! I'm here!" Outdoors, they stood a better chance of surviving the quake.

The ancient Greeks saw earthquakes as the anger of the sea god, Poseidon, particularly because tsunamis often wiped out island villages. The philosopher Aristotle blamed earthquakes on winds that blew into the planet's interior, noting that "porous soil is shaken more."

One of the first people to record and examine the evidence left behind by an earthquake was Professor John Winthrop of Harvard University. In 1755 he wrote a scientific paper describing the details of the Boston earthquake. He was at home when the quake struck and noted that he saw "one small wave of earth moving along," lifting each brick in the floor and setting it back down. He measured the flight path of bricks that fell from his chimney and calculated how long it took for a brick to fall. His paper, presented to a group of researchers in Britain, helped spark others to wonder why earthquakes happened.

In 1760 British geologist John Mitchell was the first person to correctly theorize why earthquakes occur, writing: "Earthquakes are waves set up by shifting masses of rock miles below the surface." He felt confident that the speed of seismic waves could be measured by their arrival time at distant points, and those points could be used to find the spot above the origin of the earthquake, its epicenter. Following in Mitchell's footsteps, British geologist John Milne studied

## TSUNAMI: A WALL OF WATER

Tsunamis are one of the most terrifying side effects of an earthquake. When the seafloor stretches out of shape during an earthquake, seismic waves start sloshing the sea like a bowl being shaken. This generates giant walls of water, sometimes more than 100 feet (30 meters) high, which rage against the coastline. Entire islands in the South Pacific have vanished under the force of a tsunami. These monster waves can wipe away a seaside resort, or run straight up a river and tear everything off its banks.

Alaska's 1964 earthquake created tsunamis that reached the shores of Hawaii and Japan! Since so many people are at risk of tsunamis in the Pacific Ocean, there is now a Tsunami Warning Network. In many towns in Washington and Oregon, sirens blare on a weekly basis for tsunami drills.

earthquakes in Japan. Using a seismograph—a pen attached to a pendulum device—he attempted to record the earth shaking. By 1893 he had developed a method to track the waves on film.

Each earthquake generates three different types of waves. Primary waves move through the interior of the earth, pushing particles back and forth, like a spring. Because these waves move at a constant speed for up to 7,000 miles (11,265 kilometers), they can be used to predict when the earthquake will affect a spot distant from the epicenter. Secondary waves also travel through the earth's interior but can only pass through solids. They shake particles up and down. Finally, there are surface waves, which lift the ground and set it back down again. They move particles in exactly the opposite order of a wave in water: forward, up, back, and down.

In 1902 the British Association for the Advancement of Science started an observatory for seismic surveillance. Eleven years later, forty sites watched over the earth's shaking, sending their observations to Great Britain for correlation. Today, there is a web of information collected from more than 2,500 outposts tracking seismic waves around the globe. Roughly 60,000 seismic readings are funneled each month to the U.S. Geological Survey National Earthquake Information Center. The magnitude and epicenter of each quake are calculated within the hour. Depending on the severity of the quake, alerts go out to governments, disaster relief agencies, and news services in the affected region. Whenever an earthquake alert is triggered, more than 280 pages of computer data quickly pile up!

## THE RICHTER SCALE

For many years people used a subjective estimate of earthquake damage—known as the Mercalli scale—to guess the strength of an earthquake. The scale included such measures as "some breakage of dishes" and "ground badly cracked."

In 1935 seismologist Charles F. Richter invented the Richter scale. It is a measurement of magnitude based on the amount of energy released by an earthquake. The scale starts at 1.0 and has no upper limit. Each number stands for 10 times more energy released. An earthquake at 2.0 causes little damage. North America's strongest earthquake was Alaska's Good Friday earthquake in 1964, which registered an 8.5.

## WHOSE FAULT IS IT?

Most earthquakes occur because of friction between faults in the earth's crust. Faults are weak spots in the bedrock. They may be shallow or deep, clean fractures of rock or regions of crushed stone. They can hide under layers of soil, unnoticed until they create a tremor. A fault can occur anywhere where rocks are under stress, either pushing and grinding into each other or pulling apart. This can take place on a small scale in a mine, where tunneling and rock bolts create stresses on the rocks. On the largest scale, faults ring our planet where the continental plates meet. These are the areas where seismic activity is the greatest, where the collision of plates creates massive stresses deep underground.

From the air, the San Andreas Fault in California looks like a giant scar on the landscape. It marks the spot where the Pacific Plate and the North American Plate are grinding into each other. Smaller faults branch off it like cracks in a broken mirror, such as the Hollister Fault and the Landers Fault. While the San Andreas Fault is the site of many tremors and earthquakes, it shifts about 2 inches (5 centimeters) a year. Another California fault, the Hayward Fault, also constantly releases its energy. But the town of Hayward hasn't had an earthquake since 1868. Instead, the town is slowly being pulled apart by the fault. It runs down streets, through yards, and right down the middle of Berkeley Stadium, from one goalpost to the other! Then each side of the fault slips against the other at a rate of a few millimeters a year.

To deal with the physical stress of rocks straining, a fault can do one of three things. It can slowly slide (like the Hayward Fault), releasing its energy in a constant change of shape. A fault can also build up a store of elastic energy over hundreds, or thousands, of years. This is like stretching a rubber band out as far as it will go. An earthquake occurs when the elastic energy rebounds: Let go of one end of the rubber band, and it snaps back to its original position. An earthquake occurs as a result of this "snapping back," and the faults rapidly slip past each other, settling into a less stressful position. A fault can also rupture suddenly, generating an earthquake.

Since faults can occur in the middle of continental plates, earthquakes are not limited to plate boundaries. The earthquakes at New Madrid, Missouri, during 1811 and 1812 happened in the middle of a plate. On February 7, 1812, the tremors spread out over 2 million square miles (5.2 million square kilometers). Church bells rang in Boston. Hundreds of miles of forests fell over. A large mass of land sank in Tennessee, creating Reelfoot Lake. Waterspouts shot into the air along the banks of the Mississippi River. The river even reversed its course!

The San Andreas Fault runs through much of California and has been responsible for many earthquakes, including the San Francisco earthquake in 1906 and the World Series earthquake in 1989.

The Good Friday earthquake tore apart this schoolyard in Anchorage, Alaska. It's a good thing that the 8.5 earthquake did not occur in a more populated region of the world.

Naturalist John James Audubon, riding on horseback through Kentucky, described the effect: "The ground rose and fell in successive furrows, like the ruffled waters of a lake."

Geologists eventually traced deep faults from New Madrid out toward northeastern Arkansas, Cairo, Illinois, and northwestern Tennessee.

Plate boundary quakes tend to be very strong earthquakes. Although most earthquakes last less than a minute, the Good Friday earthquake in Alaska in 1964 shook the ground for an incredible seven minutes! Its seismic waves were recorded as far away as Cape Canaveral in Florida.

## PREDICTING AN EARTHQUAKE

Is there such a thing as "earthquake weather"? People have often described an "eerie calm" just before an earthquake. Sometimes the earth itself gives premonitions: Dry springs suddenly bubble with water, and the water in clean, clear springs turns muddy. Researchers, looking though historical records, point out that earthquakes have occurred in all sorts of weather: wind, rain, sun, and snow. So there is no "special" weather that will warn of an earthquake.

Animals sometimes sense an impending earthquake. No one knows exactly why. One of the earliest records of animal response came from the ancient Greeks. Five days before an earthquake ruined the city of Helas, swarms of rats, weasels, snakes, and centipedes left the city. Dogs howled uncontrollably before the earthquake that leveled Messina, Italy, in 1783. In 1805 swarms of locusts crept into the sea at Naples, Italy, before the earthquake hit. Kodiak bears in Alaska came out of hibernation several weeks early, running from their dens, to avoid the massive earthquake that struck in 1964.

## MEASURING WITH CLAMS

During an earthquake, new land sometimes rises along a fault. To study the effects of ancient earthquakes, geologists look for clues to how much the ground has risen. One of their favorite indicators is the lowly clam. Clams like to attach themselves to rocks at sea level. By studying sea-cliff faults for clams, geologists can figure out where the shoreline used to be, and how much it rose during each known earthquake

In one cliff at Mara, Japan, biologists discovered clam holes at several elevations up to 45 feet (14 meters) high. By correlating the clam locations with historical records, they determined that quakes had lifted the land in A.D. 33, 818, 1703, and 1923. At Valparasio, Chile, Charles Darwin discovered clamshells 1,300 feet (396 meters) above sea level!

The world record for new land rising occurred so suddenly that it didn't need a clamshell measurement. In one earthquake at Disenchantment Bay, Alaska, in 1899, the coastline rose by more than 47 feet (14 meters)!

*These Japanese first-graders hide under their desks during an earthquake drill. The padded hoods are called Bosai Zukin. Schools in California have earthquake drills, too.*

After studying their own records, the Chinese tried to use such natural warnings to predict earthquakes. In 1975 they evacuated villages in Liaoning Province based on animal flight, muddy water in otherwise clear ponds, and wells bubbling with noxious gases. An earthquake struck, and thousands of lives were saved. But there were no warning signs when the next big earthquake came along, and thousands died.

## WHAT YOU CAN DO

Earthquake prediction remains an inexact science. We can never be sure when and where they will hit. If you live in an earthquake-prone region, check with your local Geological Survey for guidelines on how to be prepared for an earthquake.

When an earthquake occurs, it's safer to be outdoors in an open field, away from buildings. If you are indoors, stay away from windows and duck under a table or desk to protect yourself from falling objects.

# UNSTABLE GROUND 4

Jamaica's largest city, rowdy Port Royal, served as a base for pirates of the Caribbean to raid ships that ventured too close to their waters. Originally established as a fortress, the city grew up on a long peninsula of sand that hooked around a calm harbor. Many a pirate spent his treasure in this busy trading port, with its dozens of taverns ready for buccaneers to plot their next adventure.

Just before noon on June 7, 1692, an earthquake struck Jamaica. At Port Royal, this was no ordinary earthquake. First one tremor shook the land. People rushed out of buildings and into the unpaved streets. A second tremor hit. Below the city, the peninsula vibrated, shifted, and turned into quicksand. Whole buildings sank straight down into the sand. As thousands of people tried to flee in horror, they sank into the streets. Some people were lucky. Spouts of water from below pushed them back up like corks, and they floated to safety. But a third of the inhabitants of Port Royal died when the third tremor stopped. The sand hardened around these people who sank, suffocating them.

## LIQUID GROUND

The temporary quicksand at Port Royal is a side effect of earthquakes called soil liquefaction. It's the same phenomenon that caused buildings to sink into sandy soil in San Francisco's Marina district during the 1989 earthquake.

When you step on wet sand on a beach, you sink into it a little. The grains of sand are pressed closely enough together to support your weight, even though there are pockets of water between them. Strong vibrations, like those from an earthquake, can force more space between the grains of sand. The grains no longer stick together, so they cannot support any weight. The sand becomes quicksand, supported only by the liquid beneath it. Heavy buildings will tilt or sink into the liquid. Buried water mains, gasoline tanks, and pipelines will float. When the vibrations stop, the sand grains come back together again.

Port Royal suffered because it was built on a sandbar. San Francisco's Marina district had liquefaction because it was built on landfill, including the ruins of old buildings that had been dumped there after the 1906 San Francisco earthquake. In fact, some of the timbers from these old buildings popped back up to the surface during the 1989 earthquake! Why?

The upward pressure of water during an earthquake (which saved some people at Port Royal) can create an odd-looking spout called a sand boil, or a sand volcano. Sand sprays up in a fountain with water through cracks in the ground. So much sand can be pushed upward that it can create a mound that looks like a volcano! The pressure can be great enough to push up large objects, like the buried timbers in San Francisco. During the great New Madrid earthquakes, sand boils pushed up so much sand out of the ground that there are still places in Arkansas and Missouri where massive regions of sprayed sand can be seen from satellites orbiting the earth.

While liquefaction is often a side effect of earthquakes in coastal regions and floodplains, it is also known to occur well away from surface water. If the water table—the depth at which water collects in the ground—is close to the surface in an area with loose soil, that area may have liquefaction during an earthquake. Because of this, places as dry as Death Valley, California, show signs of ancient liquefaction!

If liquefaction happens where the ground is even slightly sloped, a landslide will occur. Port Royal, in part, slid into the sea. In 1959, under 50 feet (15 meters) of water, divers found perfectly preserved houses with walls still standing. One house still had a dinner in a kettle on the stove and plates stacked on the table! For many years, archaeologists assumed that Port Royal disappeared in a submarine landslide triggered by the earthquake. But more recent studies, which included putting together eyewitness accounts of the event, point to liquefaction as the cause of most of the city's destruction.

*The Marina district in San Francisco was especially hard-hit by the 1989 earthquake. Liquefaction of the landfill soil caused much of the damage.*

## STEPPING IN TOO DEEP

Quicksand is an unstable surface that often forms when springs push up through sand. In some springs, you can see the sand boils underwater, where water constantly keeps the sand in a bubbling motion.

Just as with liquefaction, the grains of sand are forced apart by the flow of water. Unlike liquefaction, it's a constant flow of water. The grains can never completely touch, so the sand can never support any weight.

Quicksand most often occurs in streams and rivers. It can form along the shores, in midstream, or even in a dry desert riverbed. All it takes to create quicksand are springs that are constantly keeping the sand in suspension.

*Mirror Lake at Natural Bridge in Virginia is a pool of quickclay. The dark particles suspended in water make a very reflective surface.*

Contrary to scary stories, quicksand doesn't "pull you down." Since quicksand is part water and part sand, you will sink in it just like you would in water. Then, your natural buoyancy will take over, and you will float. Still, sinking in quicksand is an unpleasant experience. Most people sink up to their necks. You will sink faster if you struggle.

Mud is unstable ground as well. It forms a nice hard, packed surface when it bakes in the sun. But let a little water get in there, and mud becomes a hazard. Water lubricates each particle of clay, making it slippery. The particles no longer stick together, and the ground gives way under your feet. Deep sticky, oozy mud is almost impossible to get out of without help.

## WHAT YOU CAN DO ABOUT QUICKSAND

If you suspect quicksand in an area that you're exploring, carry a long stick. Test the ground ahead of you to make sure it is stable. If you touch an area of sand and it rolls like waves, beware of quicksand!

If you do fall into quicksand, try to get onto your back as quickly as possible. You will be able to float better that way. Don't panic! The more you move, the quicker you sink. Once you reach your natural buoyancy point, you'll be able to float. If someone is nearby and can help you, he or she should try to reach near you with a stick or a board—something that will float—to pull you out.

## TREMBLING EARTH

The Creeks called this land O-ke-fin-o-cau (Okefenokee in English), "the land of the trembling earth." This lush, dark swamp covering about 700 square miles (1,815 square kilometers) of southern Georgia, teems with life. Herons flock to the trees, looking for tasty bullfrogs. Alligators bellow in the darkness. Large cypress trees, their roots reaching deep under the inky black water, drop leafy debris from high canopies.

The trembling earth here isn't quaking because of a tremor or an earthquake. Instead, it's a lesson in how new dry land appears in a swamp.

A swamp is not a place where you would expect to find much solid ground. In fact, when you find dry ground, there is a good chance it won't be solid at all! The slow decay that occurs at the bottom of a

*Okefenokee Swamp in Georgia has large areas of floating vegetation that look solid but would probably sink under your weight.*

swamp or a bog creates layers of partially decomposed plants, called peat. When enough peat accumulates and dries, it can form a base for other plants to grow on. If water continues to flow under the dried layer of peat, the resulting dry ground is a quaking bog. It will bounce under your feet, just like standing on a waterbed.

In the Okefenokee Swamp, mounds of floating peat support bushes and even small trees. These floating islands drift across the surface of the black water. Naturalists think that these islands are mostly made up of decayed cypress tree debris and water lilies. As the trees and bushes on each island grow larger, their roots tap deeper and eventually reach the swamp bottom. The island stops floating, because it is anchored by plant roots. But it will take many, many years before it stops quaking.

Depending on the thickness of the peat, the island may be able to support some weight: a nesting heron or an alligator. But if a person steps on it, the ground quakes, and it may sink!

Floating islands made of decomposed vegetation aren't unique to the Okefenokee Swamp. They drift through peat bogs in Ireland, through the muskeg swamps of Northern Canada, the fens of Finland, and the marshes surrounding Lake Arenal in Costa Rica. Matted masses of live vegetation also form floating islands, providing shelter to the sitatunga, an aquatic antelope in Kenya, and clogging inland waterways in Australia, India, and Singapore.

Unstable ground exists in two forms: expected and unexpected. When the ground suddenly gives way under your feet, it's not a comfortable feeling. Swamps, marshes, and bogs are full of naturally unstable ground, at least for us humans.

# WHEN THE BOTTOM DROPS OUT 5

Five thousand years ago the city of Ubar ruled the Arabian Desert. Built at a large oasis, the city attracted merchants from around the world. Its towers guarded a treasure worth more than gold—the leaves of the frankincense bush. Traders traveled dangerous desert roads to swap their goods for frankincense, which they used in their temples. Then one day, without warning, Ubar vanished from the trade route.

For hundreds of years explorers searched for the city's ruins. Finally, in the 1980s, researchers used sand-penetrating radar from the space shuttle *Challenger* to look for Ubar. Satellite images uncovered the ancient trading roads. In 1991 an expedition arrived at the village of Ash Shisur, Oman. They found an oasis and started to dig. As they uncovered the ruins beneath the sands, the archaeologists discovered why the city had disappeared so suddenly, leaving no trace.

Ubar had fallen into an enormous sinkhole!

## THE PROBLEM OF SUBSIDENCE

Subsidence is a sudden disaster that occurs when the ground caves in, leaving a gaping hole. Anything on top of the hole—trees, bushes, grass, cars, even buildings—will fall in! At Ubar, the ground under the city weakened because of a low water table. A sinkhole appeared, and the buildings fell into it, landing in the caverns below. Subsidence, in gen-

*When the ground subsided in this San Francisco neighborhood, it swallowed an entire house.*

eral, is a man-made problem. Sinkholes are the only form of natural subsidence.

When a water main breaks, the tremendous flow of water pouring out of the open pipe can eat tunnels through soft soil, setting up the scenario for subsidence. When the break is discovered and the flow of water is shut off, there is no longer anything holding up the new tunnel created by the water. The weight of roads or buildings above will collapse into the hole. In 1996 a water main break in San Francisco created a giant hole, and a large house slid into it!

Removing too much fluid from the ground can also result in subsidence and sinkholes for the same reason: The pressure of the fluid was needed to hold up the ground. The pumping of oil out of oil fields near Los Angeles has caused ground to collapse, because no water was pumped back in to replace the volume of oil that was removed. If too many wells are drilled in an area, or too much water is removed from existing wells, it can trigger subsidence. In March 1998, well drilling for a new group of homes in Tampa, Florida, caused several sinkholes to open up. One was half the length of a football field.

## MINE SUBSIDENCE

During the early twentieth century, miners didn't stop to think about the consequences of digging tunnels under the earth. They often dug through massive bodies of solid rock, using timbers to hold up the tunnels. When they abandoned a mine, it would fill with water. The timbers would rot, and the tunnels would collapse. Tunnels built for highways and railroads are reinforced with concrete and steel to prevent this sort of collapse. Even the use of rock bolts—pounded into the mine roof to squeeze the rocks together—didn't help. Eventually bolts rust, allowing the roof to cave in. It is now standard practice to leave large pillars of stone to help support the tunnel roof. Some mining companies also use waste rock to refill old tunnels.

In coal-mining regions, coal seams are mined across a broad expanse, leaving pillars of coal to support the roof. Coal seams were mined as close to the surface as they were found. The upper tunnels of some old coal mines in Pittsburgh, Pennsylvania, are less than 10 feet (3 meters) under people's basements.

Mine subsidence is a serious problem wherever people build on top of old mines, especially coal mines. If too much weight is put on the surface, the ground will cave in!

There are two types of mine subsidence. Pit subsidence is sudden, like a sinkhole. It occurs where there are fewer than 165 feet (50 meters) of soil and rock between the mine tunnels and the surface, and the surrounding rocks are mostly weak sedimentary rock. The ground caves in to the mine below, forming a crater that slopes inward like a huge drain.

Trough, or sag, subsidence is a gentle settling of the surface. It won't swallow a house, but it can crack a foundation. It is caused by the col-

47

lapse of pillars in the mine, not necessarily because of any added weight on the surface. It creates a long, low depression in the ground.

The collapse of improperly closed mine shafts is another subsidence danger. These shafts can be very deep. In 1977 one such shaft in an abandoned coal mine opened up inside a family's garage in Youngstown, Ohio. The pit was 115 feet (35 meters) deep!

## WHAT YOU CAN DO ABOUT SUBSIDENCE

People who live in places prone to mine subsidence—such as Ohio, Pennsylvania, Colorado, Iowa, and West Virginia—can check with their state Geological Survey for maps that show if mines are under their property. If your family's house is at risk, it is a good idea to have mine subsidence insurance.

## HOW SINKHOLES FORM

Sinkholes are found all over the world, in desert sands, steaming jungles, and arctic tundra. But unlike mine subsidence, sinkholes are part of a natural process, erosion. Although sinkholes appear suddenly, it takes a special set of conditions for one to happen.

Not all sinkholes have caverns under them, but sinkholes and caverns have one thing in common: They form in a type of ground called karst, which contains rocks that dissolve easily. Limestone is the most common type of karst, and it's prone to subsidence. Why? Even though it's a rock, limestone is weak.

When rain falls on the ground, it seeps through a layer of leaves and dirt. The water picks up acid from the decaying leaves. As acidic water trickles into the ground, the limestone below dissolves. Small crevices widen into big cracks. Over thousands of years cavities will grow into caverns. With cracks above and caverns below, the limestone weakens. The weak cavern ceiling may stay in place for hundreds of years. But when the roof finally collapses...

Crash! A sinkhole appears.

A collapse sinkhole often occurs because the water table is too low. If there is a drought, no rain seeps into the ground to refill the water table. If too much water is taken out of the water table through wells, the water level will drop. Since water helps to hold up weak limestone, a lower water table means that the support is missing and sinkholes can occur.

*Joyce Tanner, of Youngstown, Ohio, was understandably surprised when mine subsidence caused this old mine shaft to reopen in her garage.*

A more common type of sinkhole is the subsidence sinkhole. It occurs when rain carries dirt and sand into the cracks in the limestone. As the cracks fill with these heavier materials, the weak limestone collapses underground. A bowl-shaped depression appears in the ground above. As more dirt and sand wash into the bowl, it finally collapses under its own weight.

Boom! Another sinkhole!

In 1986, employees at a car dealership in Winter Park, Florida, didn't think much of the little subsidence sinkhole in their lot when they left one night. That little sinkhole grew quickly and gobbled up an entire city block in a day! A swimming pool, a house, a truck, and part of the car dealer's lot fell into the hole! The sinkhole eventually filled with water and is now part of a city park.

49

In 1982, over just one weekend, 200 sinkholes opened up in Ocala, Florida, after 15 inches (38 centimeters) of rain fell on the city. Sinkholes appeared in backyards, at schools, at the mall, and even in the middle of a highway! Why? The rain washed so much dirt and sand into crevices in the limestone so quickly that every weak spot collapsed.

*The residents of Winter Park, Florida, got quite a shock when this sinkhole appeared in town.*

The world's largest sinkhole appeared in Shelby County, Alabama, in 1972. It's 425 feet long, 350 feet wide, and 150 feet deep (130 by 107 by 46 meters), big enough to fit twelve football fields across the top!

This giant sinkhole was caused by nearby mining. Since mines intersect the water table, they quickly fill with water. The water has to be pumped out constantly for the miners to be able to work. This procedure, called dewatering, often triggers sinkholes. It removes so much water from the water table that the limestone weakens in many places at once. In the 1950s dewatering at a nearby mine caused dozens of sinkholes around the Hershey Chocolate Factory in Pennsylvania. In the 1960s dewatering caused a tragic disaster at a South African gold mine, where a factory building full of people fell into a giant sinkhole.

Two important facts: Sinkholes only happen in karst, and water is the prime trigger for creating a sinkhole. If there is too little water underground because of a drought, dewatering, or too many wells drilled in a karst area, then sinkholes will result. Heavy rains add water to the ground and cause sinkholes by washing dirt and sand into the weak limestone. Finally, man-made changes to natural drainage patterns can also cause sinkholes by pushing too much dirt-filled water into weak ground.

## SINKHOLES AS HABITATS

On land and under the sea, sinkholes provide shelter for plants and animals. Many of the earth's sinkholes have existed for hundreds, thousands, even millions of years. Most sinkholes occur in forests and fields, deserts and tundra, and are not a threat to people.

Sinkholes stop growing eventually. Soon, new life moves into the sinkhole. It becomes a unique part of the environment. Since the sinkhole is lower than the ground around it, temperatures in it are cooler. It will attract plants and animals that like cool, damp places, such as mosses, ferns, frogs, and lizards. When it rains, water will flow to the bottom of the sinkhole and down into the ground through a crevice known as the throat. If the throat clogs up, the sinkhole may fill with water and become a pond or lake. Many of the lakes in central Florida were once sinkholes. Or if the throat stays dry, it may uncover a secret passage to a cavern. Explorers discovered Luray Caverns in Virginia by poking around in the bottom of a sinkhole.

In some parts of the world, sinkholes are the only source of freshwater. Cenotes are sinkholes that are always full of water, because they are deep enough to reach the water table. The ancient Maya built their cities around cenotes in the Yucatán Peninsula of Mexico. In the vast Arabian Desert, water-filled sinkholes are islands of life. Each oasis attracts plants and animals around an artesian well. Natural pressure pushes the water up from underground chambers to the surface through a sinkhole. Some sinkhole springs pour out massive amounts of water, enough to create a river. Silver Springs, Florida, is the world's largest sinkhole spring, pouring out 834 million gallons (3.2 billion liters) of water each day at its maximum flow: enough water daily for three million people!

Sinkholes even appear in the ocean floor. Sinkholes known as blue holes lead to caverns deep beneath the ocean floor. Other ocean-floor sinkholes are springs pushing freshwater into the salty ocean. Fish are attracted to these undersea fountains of freshwater. Most of these ocean-floor sinkholes formed millions of years ago, when the bottom of the ocean was dry land.

## SINKHOLES AND CLEAN WATER

Because of its throat, a sinkhole acts like a drainpipe. Anything that flows into a sinkhole disappears into the water table. In some regions, sand and gravel filter the water as it trickles down to the water table. Not so in karst. Its underground crevices work just like the water pipes in your house. Anything that goes into a sinkhole directly affects the water table. And the water table is where your drinking water comes from!

In 1916 tourists came from all over for boat rides into the scenic Hidden River Cave in Kentucky. Meanwhile, the people of Hidden River were dumping sewage into the sinkholes near their homes. By the 1930s their drinking water was contaminated. By the 1940s the tourists stopped coming because the cavern stunk like a sewer and everything in it died. The good news is that, eventually, the earth heals itself. Life returned to the cave because the town stopped dumping sewage into the sinkhole many years ago.

Dumping trash into a sinkhole causes problems too. Water runs over the trash and carries nasty odors and flavors down into the drinking water. Édouard-Alfred Martel was a speleologist (cave scientist)

from France who figured this out in 1898. He proved that an outbreak of typhoid, a deadly disease, came from water running over dead animals dumped into sinkholes. That same water, full of disease, bubbled up to the surface in springs many miles away. Martel worked hard to stop sinkhole dumping in France.

## WHAT YOU CAN DO ABOUT SINKHOLES

Do you live in an area with sinkholes? Maybe. Is there limestone under your feet? Nearly 75 percent of the continental United States has the right type of ground for sinkholes. Sinkholes can be found in the deserts of New Mexico and the islands of Alaska, and all over the world, from the steaming jungles of Borneo to the hills of Ireland and the deserts of Western Australia.

Could a sinkhole swallow your school? In the 1980s, Forest High School in Ocala, Florida, frequently had problems with sinkholes opening up under buildings. One water-filled sinkhole on campus was a constant reminder that a sinkhole could appear anytime!

In 1996, a 15-foot (5-meter)-deep sinkhole appeared under the library at the Lower Allen Elementary School in Carlisle, Pennsylvania. The sinkhole formed slowly, so students had a chance to look into it before a construction crew filled the sinkhole up with rocks and clay.

Will a sinkhole affect you? Most sinkholes don't happen in backyards. When they do, the cracks in the lawn are enough warning that you should get out of the house and call for help. The Geological Survey will send someone to check the property and confirm that a sinkhole is growing and will provide other experts to take care of the problem. Sinkholes in residential areas must be filled in properly so they don't open up again.

Most important, if you live in a karst area, sinkholes can affect you by the role they play in your water supply. Are any of your landfills near sinkholes? Are people dumping old tires, trash, and washing machines into sinkholes? Are farmers spreading manure too close to sinkholes? If so, your water may be polluted. Your class can work with local authorities on projects to clean out sinkhole dumps. You can write legislators to express your concern. It's important that sinkholes are dealt with appropriately so that your drinking water stays fresh and clean.

# GLOSSARY

**avalanche:** the sudden collapse and downhill slide of a layer of snow

**bedrock:** the deep layer of rock underneath the soil

**couloir:** a known path down which avalanches frequently slide

**earthquake:** tremors that radiate from a rupture along a fault

**epicenter:** the point on the earth's surface above the earthquake's focus

**fault:** a weak spot in the bedrock

**focus:** the spot under the earth's surface where a fault ruptures

**frost heaving:** movement of soil and rock due to freezing and thawing of wet ground

**ground cover:** plants and trees that help hold down the soil

**karst:** a landscape where the bedrock (such as limestone, gypsum, and chalk) dissolves easily, allowing erosion to form caverns and sinkholes

**lahar:** muddy volcanic landslides containing ash, soil, rocks, and fluids

**landslide:** a sudden downhill flow of soil and rock

**liquefaction:** the temporary change of soil or sand to a liquid when vibrations cause water to separate each particle and make it float

**mass movement:** the downward flow of rocks and soil due to gravity

**permafrost:** a layer of permanently frozen soil

**pyroclastic flow:** a volcanic mixture of hot gases and ash that flows along the ground at high speed

**quicksand:** sand grains forced apart by water pressure

**rock glacier:** a large talus pile that flows slowly, as a glacier

**sand boil:** an explosion of sand on the earth's surface due to upward water pressure

**seismic waves:** measurable movements in the earth's crust

**sinkhole:** a depression in the earth's surface formed by either the erosion of underlying limestone or the collapse of a cavern

**soil creep:** the continual downhill movement of particles of soil due to gravity

**solifluction:** the slipping and flowing of surface layers of waterlogged soil

**subsidence:** the collapse of the earth's surface downward

**talus:** rock fragments of any size or shape that fall and pile up at the bottom of a cliff or steep rocky slope

**tsunami:** an abnormally high ocean wave generated by seismic activity

**water table:** the level underground at which water fully saturates soil and rock

# RECOMMENDED RESOURCES

## FURTHER READING

*Avalanche!* by Howard Facklam and Margery Facklam (Crestwood House, 1991)

*Earthquake* by Christopher Lampton (Millbrook Press, 1994)

*Earthquakes* by Sally M. Walker (Carolrhoda Books, 1996)

*Landslides, Slumps and Creep* by Peter Goodwin (Franklin Watts, 1997)

*The Mystery of the Bog Forest* by Lorus J. Milne and Margery Milne (Dodd, Mead, 1984)

*Our Patchwork Planet* by Helen Roney Sattler (Lothrop, Lee & Shepard Books, 1995)

*When Disaster Strikes: Earthquakes* by Karen Spies (Twenty-First Century Books, 1994).

## ON THE WORLD WIDE WEB

While the Internet is constantly evolving, these sites have been around for a while. For other related information online, try using a search engine with keywords like "earthquake," "tsunami," "landslide," "avalanche," "sinkhole," and "subsidence."

### The Cyberspace Snow and Avalanche Center

www.csac.org/

A nonprofit organization linking a network of avalanche warning centers around the world. This site offers: current avalanche conditions, information on why avalanches happen, first-person accounts of being in an avalanche, photos, and a database of avalanche incidents.

### It's Hayward's Fault

www.mcs.csuhayward.edu/~shirschf/hayward.htm

A photographic walking tour of the Hayward Fault, which is slowly pulling California towns apart. From the California State University, Hayward Campus.

### National Landslide Information Center

www.gldage.cr.usgs.gov/html_files/nlicsun.html

The U.S. Geological Survey's links to information on landslides and landslide research projects. The images section includes simulation films and photos of landslide damage.

### Susan Rosenberg's Quaking Home Page

www.earthwaves.com/quake.html

This earthquake fan has information on current quakes, prior quakes, the geology of California and why it shakes so much, how to prepare for an earthquake, and more!

### Tsunami!

www.geophys.washington.edu/tsunami/welcome.html

For general information about the dangerous waves spawned by earthquakes and submarine landslides. Includes current warnings and historical information on damage caused by tsunamis, and simulation films. From the University of Washington Geophysics program.

### USGS: Latest Earthquake Information

www.geology.usgs.gov/quake.shtml

A quick list of all earthquakes that have happened around the world in the past few days, with links to detailed information on each earthquake. From the U.S. Geological Survey.

### Virtual Earthquake

www.vflylab.calstatela.edu/edesktop/VirtApps/VirtualEarthQuake/VQuakeIntro.html

For a better understanding of how seismograms are used, you can create your own earthquake and watch the results. From California State University, Los Angeles.

# YOUR GEOLOGICAL SURVEY

Each state has its own independent Geological Survey team, which is responsible for mapping the state. They also look after geological hazards, monitor water quality and mining activity, and generally keep track of everything important about earth science where you live. And the Geological Survey is always on the scene when a natural disaster occurs. The U.S. Geological Survey has an excellent service called "Ask a Geologist" on their Website. Most states have free information available about the geological hazards in your area and information on what you can do to be prepared for a natural disaster.

**UNITED STATES GEOLOGICAL SURVEY**
U.S. Department of the Interior, U.S. Geological Survey, 508 National Center, Reston, VA 20192. www.usgs.gov/

**Alabama**
The Geological Survey of Alabama, P.O. Box O, Tuscaloosa, AL 35486-9780. PHONE: 205-349-2852. FAX: 205-349-2861. EMAIL: gsa@ogb.gsa.tuscaloosa.al.us. www.gsa.tuscaloosa.al.us

**Alaska**
State of Alaska Geological and Geophysical Surveys, 794 University Avenue, Suite 200, Fairbanks, AK 99709. PHONE: 907-451-5000. FAX: 907-451-5050. EMAIL: dggs@dnr.state.ak.us. www.dggs.dnr.state.ak.us/

**Arizona**
Arizona Geological Survey, 416 West Congress Street, Suite 100, Tucson, AZ 85701. PHONE: 520-770-3500. FAX: 520-770-3505. www.azgs.state.az.us/index.htm

**California**
California Department of Conservation, Division of Mines and Geology, 801 K Street, MS 14-33, Sacramento, CA 95814-3532. PHONE: 916-445-5716. FAX: 916-327-1853. EMAIL: dmglib@consrv.ca.gov. www.consrv.ca.gov/dmg/index.htm

**Colorado**
Colorado Geological Survey, 1313 Sherman Street, Room 715, Denver, CO 80203. PHONE: 303-866-2611. FAX: 303-866-2461. www.dnr.state.co.us/geosurvey/

**Connecticut**
Connecticut Geological and Natural History Survey, The Department of Environmental Protection, 79 Elm Street, Hartford, CT 06106-5127. PHONE: 860-424-3550. FAX: 860-424-4058. EMAIL: dep.webmaster@po.state.ct.us

**Delaware**
Delaware Geological Survey, University of Delaware, Delaware Geological Survey Building, Newark, DE 19716-7501. PHONE: 302-831-2833. EMAIL: DGS@mvs.udel.edu. www.udel.edu/dgs/dgs.html

**Florida**
Florida Geological Survey, 903 West Tennessee Street, Tallahassee, FL 32304-7700. PHONE: 850-488-9380. FAX: 850-488-8086. www.dep.state.fl.us/geo/

**Georgia**
Georgia Geological Survey, Room 400, 19 M.L. King Jr. Drive, SW, Atlanta, GA 30334. PHONE: 404-656-3214. FAX: 404-657-8379. www.dnr.state.ga.us/dnr/environ/branches/geosurv/

**Hawaii**
Hawaii Division of Water and Land Development, P.O. Box 373, Honolulu, HI 96809. PHONE: 808-587-0230. FAX: 808-587-0283. www.kumu.icsd.hawaii.gov/dlnr/Welcome.html

**Idaho**
Idaho Geological Survey, Morrill Hall, Room 332, University of Idaho, Moscow, ID 83844-3014. PHONE: 208-885-7991.

EMAIL: igs@uidaho.edu.
www.uidaho.edu/igs/igs.html

### Illinois
Illinois State Geological Survey, 615 East Peabody, Champaign, IL 61820. PHONE: 217-333-4747. www.isgs.uiuc.edu/isgshome.html

### Indiana
Indiana Geological Survey, 611 North Walnut Grove, Bloomington, IN 47401. PHONE: 812-855-1337. FAX: 812-855-7636. EMAIL: igsinfo@indiana.edu. www.adamite.igs.indiana.edu/index.htm

### Iowa
Iowa Department of Natural Resources, Energy and Geological Resources Division, Geological Survey Bureau, 109 Trowbridge Hall, Iowa City, IA 52242-1319. PHONE: 319-335-1575. FAX: 319-335-2754. www.igsb.uiowa.edu/

### Kansas
Kansas Geological Survey, University of Kansas, 1930 Constant Avenue, Lawrence, KS 66047-3726. PHONE: 785-864-3965. FAX: 785-864-5317. www.kgs.ukans.edu/kgs.html

### Kentucky
Kentucky Geological Survey, 228 Mining and Mineral Resources Building, University of Kentucky, Lexington, KY 40506-0107. PHONE: 606-257-5500. FAX: 606-257-1147. www.uky.edu/KGS/home.htm

### Louisiana
Louisiana Department of Natural Resources, Office of Mineral Resources, Geological And Engineering Division, P.O. Box 2827, Baton Rouge, LA 70821-2827. PHONE: 504-342-4433. www.dnr.state.la.us/MIN/GEOENG/geoeng.ssi

### Maine
Maine Geological Survey, Department of Conservation, 22 State House Station, Augusta, ME 04333-0022. PHONE: 207-287-2801. EMAIL: nrimc@state.me.us. www.state.me.us/doc/nrimc/nrimc.htm

### Maryland
Maryland Geological Survey, 2300 St. Paul Street, Baltimore, MD 21218. PHONE: 410-554-5500. www.mgs.dnr.md.gov/

### Massachusetts
Massachusetts Executive Office of Environmental Affairs, 100 Cambridge Street, 20th Floor, Boston, MA 02202. PHONE: 617-727-5830, Ext. 305. FAX: 617-727-2754. www.state.ma.us/mepa

### Michigan
State of Michigan Department of Environmental Quality, Geological Survey Division Staff Offices, P.O. Box 30256, 735 East Hazel Street, Lansing, MI 48909-7756. PHONE: 517-334-6907. FAX: 517-334-6038. www.deq.state.mi.us/gsd/

### Minnesota
Minnesota Geological Survey, 2642 University Avenue West, St. Paul, MN 55114-1057. PHONE: 612-627-4780. FAX: 612-627-4778. EMAIL: mgs@gold.tc.umn.edu. www.geolab.geo.umn.edu/mgs/

### Mississippi
Mississippi Office of Geology, P.O. Box 20307, Jackson, MS 39289-1307. PHONE: 601-961-5500. FAX: 601-961-5521. www.deq.state.ms.us/domino/deqweb.nsf

### Missouri
Missouri Department of Natural Resources, Division of Geology and Land Survey, P. O. Box 250, Rolla, MO 65402. PHONE: 1-800-334-6946. EMAIL: dnrdgls@mail.dnr.state.mo.us. www.dnr.state.mo.us/dgls/homedgls.htm

### Montana
Montana Bureau of Mines & Geology, Montana Tech, 1300 West Park Street, Butte, MT 59701-8997. PHONE: 406-496-4167. FAX: 406-496-4551. EMAIL: pubsales@mbmgsun.mtech.edu. www.mbmgsun.mtech.edu/

### Nebraska
The Nebraska Natural Resources

Commission, 301 Centennial Mall South, Lincoln, NE 68509. PHONE: 402-471-2081. FAX: 402-471-3132. www.nrc.state.ne.us/

### Nevada
Nevada Bureau of Mines and Geology, University of Nevada, Reno, NV 89557-0088. PHONE: 702-784-6691, Ext. 2. FAX: 702-784-1709. EMAIL: info@nbmg.unr.edu. www.nbmg.unr.edu/

### New Hampshire
New Hampshire Department of Environmental Services, P.O. Box 2008, Concord, NH 03302-2008. PHONE: 603-271-3406. FAX: 603-271-7894. www.state.nh.us/des/descover.htm

### New Jersey
New Jersey Geological Survey, P.O. Box 427, 29 Arctic Parkway, Trenton, NJ 08625-0427. PHONE: 609-292-1185. FAX: 609-633-1004. www.state.nj.us/dep/njgs/

### New Mexico
New Mexico Bureau of Mines and Mineral Resources, 801 Leroy Place, Socorro, NM 87801. PHONE: 505-835-5410. FAX: 505-835-6333. www.geoinfo.nmt.edu/

### New York
New York State Geological Survey, 3140 Cultural Education Center, Empire State Plaza, Albany, NY 12230. PHONE: 518-474-5816. FAX: 518-473-8496. www.nysm.nysed.gov/geology.html

### North Carolina
North Carolina Geological Survey, P.O. Box 27687, Raleigh, NC 27611-7687. PHONE: 919-733-2423. FAX: 919-733-0900. www.ehnr.state.nc.us/EHNR/DLR/ncgeology/Default.htm

### North Dakota
North Dakota Geological Survey, 600 East Boulevard Avenue, Bismarck, ND 58505-0840. PHONE: 701-328-8000. FAX: 701-328-8010. www.state.nd.us/ndgs/NDGS.HomePage.html

### Ohio
Ohio Geological Survey, 4383 Fountain Square Drive, Columbus, OH 43224-1362. PHONE: 614-265-6576. EMAIL: geo.survey@dnr.state.oh.us. www.dnr.ohio.gov/odnr/geo_survey/

### Oklahoma
Oklahoma Geological Survey, 100 East Boyd, Room N-131, Norman, OK 73019-0628. PHONE: 405-325-3031; 800-330-3996. FAX: 405-325-7069. EMAIL: ogssales@ou.edu. www.ou.edu/special/ogs-pttc/

### Oregon
Oregon Department of Geology and Mineral Industries, 800 Northeast Oregon Street, Suite 965, Portland, OR 97232. PHONE: 503-731-4100. FAX: 503-731-4066. www.sarvis.dogami.state.or.us/

### Pennsylvania
Pennsylvania Topographical & Geological Survey, Department of Conservation & Natural Resources, P.O. Box 8453, Harrisburg, PA 17105-8453. PHONE: 717-787-2169. www.dcnr.state.pa.us/topogeo/index.htm

### Puerto Rico
Puerto Rico Bureau of Geology, Department of Natural and Environmental Resources, Box 9066600, Puerta de Tierra, PR 00906. PHONE: 787-722-2526. FAX: 787-723-4255

### Rhode Island
Office of Rhode Island State Geologist, Department of Geology, The University of Rhode Island, Kingston, RI 02881. PHONE: 401-874-2265. FAX: 401-874-2190 www.url.edu/cels/gel

### South Carolina
South Carolina Geological Survey, 5 Geology Road, Columbia, SC 29210. PHONE: 803-896-7708. FAX: 803-896-7695. www.water.dnr.state.sc.us/geology/geology-info.html

### South Dakota
South Dakota Geological Survey, 414 East Clark, Akeley Science Center, Vermillion, SD

57069. PHONE: 605-677-5227. FAX: 605-677-5895. www.sdgs.usd.edu/

## Tennessee
Tennessee Division of Geology, 401 Church Street, Nashville, TN 37243-0445.
PHONE: 615-532-1500. FAX: 615-532-1517
www.state.tn.us/environment

## Texas
Texas Bureau of Economic Geology, Mail: University Station, Box X, Austin, TX 78713-8924. PHONE: 512-471-1534. FAX: 512-471-0140. EMAIL: begmail@begv.beg.utexas.edu. www.utexas.edu/research/beg/

## Utah
Utah Geological Survey, P.O. Box 146100, Salt Lake City, UT 84114-6100. PHONE: 801-537-3300. FAX: 801-537-3400. www.ugs.state.ut.us/

## Vermont
Vermont Geological Survey, 103 South Main Street, Laundry Building, Waterbury, VT 05671-0301. PHONE: 802-241-3608. FAX: 802-241-3273.
www.anr.state.vt.us/geology/vgshmpg.htm

## Virginia
Virginia Division of Mineral Resources, P.O. Box 3667, Charlottesville, VA 22903. PHONE: 804-293-5121. FAX: 804-293-2239

## Washington
Washington State Department of Natural Resources, Division of Geology and Earth Resources, P.O. Box 47007, Olympia, WA 98504-7007. PHONE: 360-902-1450. FAX: 360-902-1785.
www.wa.gov/dnr/htdocs/ger/ger.html

## West Virginia
West Virginia Geological & Economic Survey, P.O. Box 879, Morgantown, WV 26507-0879. PHONE: 1-800-WV-GEOLOGY (1-800-984-3656). FAX: 304-594-2575. www.wvgs.wvnet.edu/

## Wisconsin
Wisconsin Geological and Natural History Survey, 3817 Mineral Point Road, Madison, WI 53705-5100. PHONE: 608-262-1705. FAX: 608-262-8086. www.uwex.edu/wgnhs/

## Wyoming
Wyoming State Geological Survey, Box 3008, Laramie, WY 82071. PHONE: 307-766-2286. FAX: 307-766-2605. EMAIL: wsgs@wsgs.uwyo.edu.
www.wwrc.uwyo.edu/wrds/wsgs/wsgs.html

## GEOLOGICAL SURVEY OF CANADA
Geological Survey of Canada, 601 Booth Street, Ottawa, ON K1A 0E8. PHONE: 613-996-3919. FAX: 613-943-8742. EMAIL: info-ottawa@gsc.nrcan.gc.ca.
www.nrcan.gc.ca/gsc/index_e.html

## Divisions:
Geological Survey of Canada, 3303-33rd Street N.W., Calgary, AB T2L 2A7. PHONE: 403-292-7000. FAX: 403-292-5377. EMAIL: info-calgary@gsc.nrcan.gc.ca.
www.nrcan.gc.ca/gsc/calgary/gsccalhp.htm

Geological Survey of Canada, Quebec Geoscience Centre, 2535 Boulevard Laurier C.P. 7500, Sainte-Foy, QUE G1V 4C7. PHONE: 418-654-2604. FAX: 418-654-2615. EMAIL: info-stefoy@gsc.nrcan.gc.ca.
www.nrcan.gc.ca/gsc/gscque_e.html

Geological Survey of Canada Atlantic Division, P.O. Box 1006, Dartmouth, NS B2Y 4A2. PHONE: 902-426-3225. FAX: 902-426-1466. EMAIL: info-dartmouth@gsc.nrcan.gc.ca.
www.bio.ns.ca/index.html

Geological Survey of Canada Pacific Division, 9860 West Saanich Road, Sidney, BC V8L 4B2. PHONE: 250-363-6500. FAX: 250-363-6565. EMAIL: info-sidney@gsc.nrcan.gc.ca.
www.pgc.nrcan.gc.ca/

Geological Survey of Canada Pacific Division, Suite 1600, 605 Robson Street, Vancouver, BC V6B 5J3. PHONE: 604-666-0529. FAX: 604-666-1124. EMAIL: info-vancouver@gsc.nrcan.gc.ca.
ww.nrcan.gc.ca/ess/gscpacific/vancouver/gscvanhp.htm

# INDEX